To Carole,
with best wishes,
Co...

HOW TO BOOST YOUR IMMUNE SYSTEM

Jennifer Meek

Edited by Patrick Holford

THE nutrition CONNECTION

First published in 1988
by ION Press, a division of The Institute for Optimum Nutrition
5 Jerdan Place, London SW6 1BE

Cover Design: Chris Quayle
Editor: Patrick Holford

ISBN 1 87097 600 2

Printed and bound in Great Britain by
Brier Press, High Wycombe, Bucks

CONTENTS

ARE YOU IMMUNE? 7

How immune power improves your health 8
Why immune diseases are on the increase 9
How strong is your immune system? 14

UNDERSTANDING YOUR IMMUNE SYSTEM 17

The immune battleground 17
Immune battle tactics 22

BOOSTING YOUR IMMUNE POWER 27

The immune power diet 27
How nutrients boost the immune system 31
Supplements for immune strength 39

Index 48

ABOUT THE AUTHOR

Photo courtesy of Evening Echo Bournemouth

Jennifer Meek started her career in the field of microbiology at Reading University, where she began to specialise in immunology, the study of the immune system. She continued her research into immunity at Sussex University and Bristol Medical School.

When working in the tropics she became increasingly convinced that a lot of the infectious diseases and disabilities were the consequence of a deficient diet. When she returned to Britain she remained convinced that diet was the underlying cause for many of our common health problems.

In 1984 she trained with the Institute for Optimum Nutrition and, two years later, qualified as a nutrition consultant. She now practises in Dorset, lectures throughout the country and writes for a number of publications. She is married, with two children.

CHAPTER ONE

ARE YOU IMMUNE?

IN youth and sometimes in middle age, it is easy to fool yourself into believing that all those degenerative and life-threatening diseases only happen to other people. Well, beware, you are not immune to their attacks, unless you are taking positive preventative steps. The good news is that you can improve your immune system. Your life is in your hands.

You are unique, there is no one else quite like you; not only that, but if you don't like yourself as you are - your general shape, your personality, your attitude to life, your resistance to disease - you have the ability to change it, within obvious limits. All you need is the will to do it and the knowledge of how to do it. This booklet aims to show you how to improve your immune system and how to keep it and you fighting fit.

WHO ARE YOUR ENEMIES?

Your immune system is your personal Ministry of Defence. It covers your entire body and defends you against your enemies. It also acts as a waste disposal service, clearing up all your dead cells and other unwanted rubbish.

We have many enemies in our modern world, some of which we have control over, others which we do not. To maintain the integrity of your body you need a complete and disciplined immune army, well equipped with the correct and sufficient weapons to deal with all the problems effectively.

As in any war, the fewer enemies you have attacking you at any one time, the more likely you are to remain in control and win your battles. Eliminate or reduce as many of the following enemies as you can and look for any others which may be specific for you, for example, any occupational hazard.

Smoke (tobacco and other); stress; pollution (cars, aeroplanes, industry etc.); pesticides; radiation; carcinogenic chemicals (industrial and domestic); drugs (legal, illegal and medicinal, usually requiring medical supervision for reduction or elimination, DO NOT TRY IT ALONE); food additives (especially artificial colours and flavours); incorrect balance of foods (e.g. too much salt, fat, sugar); accidents; obesity or starvation (including some dangerous forms of dieting); poor mineral balance; poor vitamin balance; inappropriate exercise; genetic defect; infections (from bacteria, viruses, fungi, protozoa, worms etc.); negative attitudes to life; unhappiness.

These are some of our main enemies and we cannot avoid them all. The best we can do is to reduce as many as possible and boost our immune system to cope with the rest.

REASONS FOR BOOSTING YOUR IMMUNE SYSTEM

1) Your immune system determines how fast you age.
2) Your immune system fights off the viruses, bacteria and other organisms which try to attack you and cause illness, from the common but irritating ones, like the common cold and thrush, to the more rare but often deadly ones like Legionnaire's disease and AIDS.
3) Your immune system has the power to destroy cancer cells as they are formed.
4) Your immune system empties your body's dustbin every

day, getting rid of dead cells, dead invaders, and toxic chemicals.
5) Your immune system offers protection from radiation and chemical pollutants.
6) If you do not look after your immune system it could lose control and actually cause allergy problems or autoimmune diseases like arthritis.
7) With a struggling immune system you are ill more often, more seriously, for more days of your life.
8) With a strong immune system you are almost invincible and should be able to lead a long, healthy and active life.

WHY DOES YOUR IMMUNE SYSTEM NEED EXTRA HELP NOW?

Incidences of immune-related diseases are increasing rapidly. There is not a person in this country today whose immune system is not being adversely affected by the unnatural pressures put upon it. The human body is marvellously adaptable but it needs time to change. We are not giving it that time.

We have changed our food, air, water, movement, in fact our whole way of living, within the passage of a few years. We expect our bodies to adapt quickly, to find ways of disposing of or storing safely, all of the new waste substances it comes across. Every new food additive, chemical pesticide, domestic detergent or drug has to be detoxified within us if it is to do no harm.

Nutrients found naturally in our food are often no longer sufficient to allow our immune system to cope effectively with the increasing problems. Ironically at this period in history, we need less food, to counteract the almost national disease of obesity, but more nutrients to help us to cope with the extra pollution and stress. We are however, busily processing nutrients out of food and eating far too much of the deficient products.

HOW CAN YOU HELP YOUR IMMUNE SYSTEM?

There are many ways in which we can help our immune system to stay fit and healthy, so reducing our susceptibility to premature ageing and disease. The master key for all of them is BALANCE. To be out of balance in any area is to tip the scales of life against us.

For ease of discussion, we have to divide things up and even leave some things out, but it should be remembered that it is the person as a whole that counts and all of our systems are interrelated and dependent on one another for the healthy functioning of the whole.

IMMUNE POWER NEEDS MOVEMENT

We have a network of tubes throughout our bodies called the lymphatic system. It is very similar to the blood system, but whereas the latter has a heart to keep the blood moving, the lymphatic system relies on muscular contractions throughout the body to keep the lymph moving.

As the lymph contains a vast proportion of our immune army, it is obviously important to keep it on the move. The human body was designed to move and too much sitting at a desk or watching the T.V. needs to be balanced with sufficient exercise to keep us as a whole and our immune system in particular, active. It should also be remembered that too much exercise can also suppress the immune system. Every body is different and requires different levels of exercise. The golden rules are: to warm up slowly, to stop if it hurts and try again later, to exercise little and often, and improve the standard gradually. There's a lot you can do to increase your exercise level without even exercising. Use the stairs rather than the lift. Shop with a basket rather than a trolley. Be active around the house, rather than relying on remote controls and labour saving kitchen gadgets.

Sleep is the time when growth hormone is released (even in adults) and this hormone stimulates the thymus, so renewing, repairing and rejuvenating your cells. It is also the time when toxins, accumulated throughout the day are dissipated. Balance sleep, exercise and rest for optimum immunity.

IMMUNE POWER AND THE MIND

Just as enough rest and sleep are necessary for us to have energy for exercise, while exercise helps us to rest and achieve sound sleep, so the condition of the mind affects the body and the condition of the body affects the mind.

We all have problems which make us feel sad, trapped, uncertain, worried, angry, fearful, unhappy, unable to cope and so on, and these feelings stimulate the release of hormones, some of which are powerful immuno-suppressants. It is well known that after bereavement, for example, the immune system is suppressed and this is often the time that a person will become ill, adding to their problems.

If we are depressed, our immune system is suppressed. If the unpleasant stressor can be removed, this is helpful, but there are many stressors that we have to live with. We need to acquire the ability to let go of negative thoughts and emotions and the best way of doing that is to replace them with positive ones.

All of us, regardless of age or condition, require goals, aims in life which give a sense of purpose and satisfaction, which build up confidence, restore enthusiasm and stimulate our immune system.

It is essential to replace the feeling of being unable to cope, as this depresses *N.K. (natural killer) cell* activity and their job is to remove any cancer cells which occur in the body every day.

The B vitamins are very helpful when in this situation; they are used up during stress, and replenishing them restores some confidence. People need and are needed by other people. A healthy personality has usually balanced time spent doing things with and for other people with time spent alone. Mind, body and spirit need to be in balance, although there is some room for variation. Like a tripod with uneven legs, you may still stand, but with a wobble!

THE NUTRITION CONNECTION

The food we eat is used up in exercise, and determines how well we sleep. It affects our thoughts, behaviour, mood and temper. It alters our hormones, skin, blood, organs, bones, muscles, fat. In short it provides the building blocks for all of our body chemistry and hence for us. We can build ourselves a shack or a castle. Roughly speaking we change our bodies almost entirely throughout a seven year period. Whatever you have now, you can improve on during that time, or, alternatively, allow it to rot, crumble, fall into disuse and disrepair. Refined, processed, nutrient deficient foods give us inferior building blocks in the form of 'empty' calories and artificial chemicals which may enable us to build a large house, but it isn't strong and things inside it don't work properly. It only takes a little wolf to huff and puff to blow the house down and expose our unhealthy bacon.

We also use food as materials for making weapons for our immune army and its quality determines whether we use water pistols or nuclear weapons to deter and defeat the enemies.

There are two main groups of people who are at risk. Together they make up a large proportion of the world's population. They are the needy and the greedy. These people suffer with malnutrition. They either do not have enough to eat or they eat far too much of nutrient-deficient foods. All foods need specific nutrients to utilise them properly and a lot of food without these nutrients puts strain on the body's laboratories. Both conditions contribute to a suppressed immune system.

MY RECIPE FOR A SOUND IMMUNE SYSTEM

Assuming that you are not on any special diet for medical reasons, these basic guidelines will serve you daily for the rest of your life.

**Of the total calorific intake, 60% should be taken in the carbohydrate form comprising grains other than exclusively wheat (our national addiction) and lots of fresh fruit and vegetables.*

**No more than 20% should come from fat, making sure that this contains the essential fatty acids especially linoleic acid (e.g. sunflower and safflower oils) and EPA (seafood and cod liver oil).*

**The remaining 20% should come from protein (ensuring all of the amino acids, if vegetarian).*

**Mix with care and cook only when necessary. Eat only when hungry. Avoid the use of seasonings such as artificial chemicals or salt. Sprinkle liberally with herbs. Which herbs, you may ask?*

H for humour many people forget it at the back of the cupboard.
E for enthusiasm we all have it but often lose it.
E for exercise we all need it but often neglect it.
E for encouragement we should all give it and receive it.
R for right thinking a positive attitude to problems.
R for relaxation to balance stress
B for balance the key to health but difficult to achieve all of the time.
S for sociability people need people.
S for supplements to make up for nutrients missing in your diet or to counteract any toxic ones put in.

HOW STRONG IS YOUR IMMUNE SYSTEM?

Are you often ill?
Do you often feel tired, lacking energy?
Do you have any allergy problems?
Do you take drugs/medicines?
Are you dependent on cigarettes, coffee or alcohol?
Do you heal slowly?
Are you unhappy with any major aspect of your life?
Do you find difficulty mixing with other people?
Do you feel isolated or trapped?
Do you get upset easily (angry, anxious, irritable etc.)?
Do you eat a lot of refined or convenience foods?
Do you rarely eat raw fruit/vegetables?
Do you eat a lot of processed snack foods in between or instead of meals?
Are you unsure of what supplements you need?
Do you take very little exercise?
Have you had any major changes in life recently?

The more times you had to answer positively the more help your immune system will need at this moment in time.

BODY LANGUAGE

It's your body, it's been with you since before you were born, yet how well do you know it? How well do you communicate with it? Just as we all have different fingerprints, so too do we all have different nutritional requirements and different early warning signs. Your body will tell you if it is getting too many toxic minerals or not enough nutritional ones. It will tell you if it is under stress, not getting enough exercise or sleep, or when you are being invaded by viruses or bacteria, but do you understand what it is telling you? Do you do anything about it?

The message is to get to know what the usual you is like and to be aware of any slight symptoms which are different for you. When the attack or insult is only slight, the symptoms will be mild, as the attack becomes more persistent or aggressive, so the strength of the symptoms will increase. How loud does your immune system have to shout before you take any notice? The earlier you recognise the symptoms, the faster you can take corrective action and the more likely you are to avert or win the battle. There are far too many subtle changes to note in a booklet of this size. Use the below as a guideline of what to look for and add symptoms peculiar to you to the list. Get to know yourself, it's the longest-lasting relationship that you can ever have!

HEAD TO TOES - EARLY WARNING SIGNS

Have you noticed any changes in the following?

Hair - fall, greasy, dry, texture, colour, growth,
Head - dull ache, foggy, floaty, sharp pain on movement, dizziness,
Skin - spots, rashes, colour change, dry, flaky, blotchy, moles, hair, dull, tight, body odour,
Eyes - yellowed whites, bloodshot, itchy, scratchy, dull, pain on movement, watery,
Ears - noises, bubbles, itchy, painful, sounds far away, own voice loud,
Nose - runny, itchy, sore, full, loss of smell, difficulty breathing,
Mouth - bad taste, bad breath, coated tongue, ulcers, loss of taste, bleeding gums,
Throat - itchy, sore, painful, swollen glands, difficulty swallowing,
Digestive tract - indigestion, gas, burning, bloatedness, pain, constipation, diarrhoea,
Nails - ridged, brittle, white spots, blue, split,
Joints - stiffness, weakness, tremors, swelling, pain,
Sleep - poor, broken, restless, sweating, dreams, heavy,
Energy level - up, down, short spurts, dependent on food intake, coffee, or other stimulants,
Mood change - up, down, depressed, elated, sad, happy, irritable, frustrated,
Food - ravenously hungry, off food, cravings.

CHAPTER TWO

UNDERSTANDING YOUR IMMUNE SYSTEM

THE whole of your body is an immune battle ground, but fighting usually occurs in one of your 6 basic areas at a time; that is, if it is possible for your immune system to confine it. If you can picture your body shape as a star, you have the five points and the centre, i.e. the head, the central core, upper left body and arm, upper right body and arm, lower left body and leg, lower right body and leg.

The master gland of the immune system is the thymus, situated in the chest. It is very active around birth, but begins to decrease in size from puberty onwards. Your pituitary gland, liver, spleen, adrenal glands, tonsils, appendix and Peyer's patches in the intestine, also play a part.

Throughout the body run the blood vessels and also the lymphatic system. The lymphatic vessels are the main distributors of the men and weapons for your immune army. It also has strategically placed nodes for specific battles, hence the enlarged glands in the neck or under the arms, or in the groin, when there is an infection present.

The whole network of lymphatic vessels and associated organs is sometimes referred to as the *reticulo endothelial system* or R.E.S. for short.

YOUR IMMUNE CELL ARMY

You are capable of synthesising over 2,000 new immune cells every second when you are in good working order, and that is quite some fighting force. It would be an effective deterrent, if bacteria had any brains!

Red blood cells (erythrocytes)

These are the most common little star ships. Their main function is to deliver oxygen to all parts of the body, but whilst they are on their rounds they keep a sharp look-out for any foreign vessels. They have "docking points" on their surface and can arrest invaders and take them to more senior members of the immune system to be dealt with.

White blood cells (leucocytes)

These are the major fighting force. However, just as our country has an army, navy and air force, we can divide our white blood cells into macrophages, polymorphs, T lymphocytes and B lymphocytes. We will consider them in turn.

Macrophages

The macrophages can be likened to transformers as they can change their form and function to suit the occasion. (We now know that the *monocytes* in the blood are the same as macrophages in the tissues.) They are flexible enough to change their shape and squeeze through blood vessel walls when they need to. There are also some macrophages which are fixed to their posts and do not move around at all.
They have receptors on their surface for recognising invaders, our own dead or defective cells and other rubbish, not

classified as self. Macrophages provide themselves with breakfast, lunch and dinner by "eating" any of these that they come across. The name for this method of disposal is *phagocytosis* and comprises ingestion, digestion and elimination of offending substances. (Occasionally they find their prey too indigestible and have to call on the T cells for help.)

These strong and ruthless defenders also have a houseproud attitude to their work and clean and tidy the blood, lymph and tissues like efficient, selective vacuum cleaners.

Macrophages are also capable of making at least 40 different enzymes and immune proteins needed for the destruction of enemies, while their peace-time activities include making enzymes necessary for clotting of the blood and for fat transport. Even in death, the macrophage is useful, as it is broken down, cannibal-style, by other macrophages and used as food.

Polymorph

This is a much smaller cell with the very long and grand title of *poly-morphonuclear neutrophile* (polymorph or pmn. for short). Its robot-like action is reminiscent of Doctor Who's dalek; programmed to seek, recognise and destroy; with only one aim in life......."I will ex-ter-min-ate".

Its enthusiasm to comply is almost invariably suicidal and it rarely lives to fight another battle. Inside the polymorph are little sealed bags called *lysosomes.* These are broken when it needs to exterminate. The enzymes inside bleach the alien to death, but unfortunately for our little robots, the enzymes are usually strong enough to digest them as well.

T lymphocytes

These are rather like rockets. Some just cruise around on surveillance duty, others have deadly warheads, but they all have to be programmed by passing through your master computer, the thymus, before they are released. There are 4 main types of T cell.

1. The *T helper cell* helps other members of the immune army. It is the body's safeguard against mistakes. If there is a possible invader of questionable identity, this T cell is called in to help and has the final say. It is also responsible for verifying an invasion and switching the immune system on to red alert.

2. The *T suppressor cell* is there to switch off the immune system when an infection has passed and you have recovered.

3. Unlike the other two, *Cytotoxic T cells* are true rockets, complete with destructive powers. Their special duty is to search out viruses and other invaders which have hidden inside your cells (which they do for protection, so that most of the immune soldiers come across these cells and recognise them as self, not knowing that there is a traitor within). They contain very strong enzyme missiles, which break up and destroy the infected cells.

4. *Lymphokine-producing T cells,* have missiles that kill, but they are directed at invaders which move in between your cells. They increase the activity of the macrophages as there are a lot of dead bodies and so much rubbish to clear up after the chemical warfare.

B lymphocytes

This type of white cell is very specific. Other members of the immune army work with the B cell, when they have problems and sometimes it acts alone. It takes an invading bug into the tissues and there interrogates it, finding out its exact shape and size, and then tailor-makes a strait-jacket that will fit that kind of bug and no other. It then gets a factory production line going and makes thousands more like it. These strait-jackets are called *antibodies*. They search out their targets and attach to them like guided missiles. The invader becomes harmless and safe until a macrophage or polymorph comes along to devour it.

B cells have "memories" and can often "remember" what shape antibody to make to tie up a specific invader e.g. chickenpox bug. This means that if we become infected with that bug again, our immune system already knows how to deal with it and all that interrogation time is saved. The invader can be dealt with much more quickly and effectively and we often don't get ill at all, or only have mild symptoms. If we do get an illness like this a second time, it means that our immune system is below par and needs a boost.

There are also less specific antibodies in the blood all of the time. They have one of 5 basic patterns, and are known as IgA, IgD, IgE, IgG and IgM. These are used for day to day running. For example, IgA is not very specific at all and doesn't have a memory; it works mainly in the gut, respiratory and genito-urinary tracts, where there is a lot of exposure to foreign substances. It needs to be non-specific or else every time we ate a new food we would become irrevocably sensitised and not be able to eat that food again. IgE is responsible for all the allergic reactions - hives, rashes, itching, rhinitis and so on. Some people inherit the tendency to make a lot of it and hence are more prone to allergies.

OTHER WEAPONS WE USE

We have considered the weapons used by our defending cells, the B lymphocytes' antibodies, and the T lymphocytes' lethal enzymes as well as the enzymes used during phagocytosis by the macrophages and polymorphs. We do have a few other tricks up our sleeves.

Interferons are a group of proteins which are present in the blood all of the time. They are inactive until stimulated by an invading virus or some types of cancer cell. When they are so stimulated, they become active and cause the cells around to produce proteins which prevent replication of the viral nucleic acid.

Complement proteins are a group of proteins which circulate in the blood. When an invader bumps into and stimulates a complement protein, it will alter chemically and attract other complement proteins to it. When 4-6 complements are joined together in a special order, the jigsaw is complete and the invader is killed. The jigsaw has to be fitted in the correct order for weapons to be released; this prevents the continuous, indiscriminate firing of weapons, so protecting your cells.

IMMUNE BATTLE TACTICS

Our skin is our first obvious line of defence and works well to keep water, bugs, chemicals and radiation out or, at least, to a minimum, as long as it remains intact. Areas which are not protected by skin have mucous membranes or other methods of getting rid of unwanted irritants. Coughing, sneezing, crying, mucus production, production of faeces, salivating, all get rid of foreign or toxic substances.

Sufficient levels of zinc in seminal and amniotic fluid keep these free from harmful bugs, and lysozyme, an enzyme in the blood, eyes, mouth and nose helps to protect against invading bacteria, whilst interferons tackle the viruses. On the skin and in the stomach, acid conditions prevent a lot of attacks, as do the bile salts and fatty acids in the intestines.

When bugs do manage to penetrate our exterior, they are bathed in the antibacterial lysozyme and antiviral interferons, which will be activated as long as there is enough manganese and vitamin C present. If these are not effective, they are met by the phagocytic cells (macrophages and polymorphs). These cells need to contain 20 micrograms of vitamin C per 100 million cells or they cannot digest their foe. Vitamin C also increases their motility.

Complement proteins may also be stimulated to come together and destroy the invader, but they require sufficient calcium, magnesium and vitamin C in order to do this.

Vitamin C increases the number of lymphocytes, which in turn increases the number of antibodies and destructive enzymes that can be produced.

As a last resort, if the body cannot get rid of the offending substance it builds little walls of macrophages around it to keep it from causing damage. These walls are constantly being replaced.

VACCINATION

We can acquire immunity to certain bugs by killing them or altering them in some way so that they cannot cause disease, and then injecting a small amount into the body. The B cells make antibodies to the bug and remember how to do it so that if we meet the infectious agent again in the future, there is no delay in killing it fast, before it has time to get a hold. We either avoid the disease altogether or get a milder form, just as when we have had the disease before. This is what vaccination is all about.

Unfortunately, some bugs, like the virus that causes the flu, and the AIDS virus, have a clever habit of changing their surface slightly so that the antibody doesn't fit, and it is therefore very difficult to get a vaccine for this type of bug.

DISTINGUISHING FRIEND FROM FOE

You now know your battleground, the invaders, the defenders and their weapons, but how do the defenders know what to attack and what to protect? It's no good having a strong, well-equipped army that shoots everything in sight! The answer lies with your master computer, the thymus. Since before you were born it has been giving all your cells an "identity disc" and a code, which is recorded in its memory banks.

A language analogy helps the understanding of what goes on. Think of your body as your country. Every individual cell has been taught to speak the same language - English. We can immediately recognise someone from a different country, if they speak a different language. Your immune army would arrest these and destroy them.

There are two obvious loopholes. A French person may come into your country and speak perfect English. This can happen when a virus gets into the body and then hides inside one of our cells. Our immune cells recognise the English and leave it alone, but the cytotoxic T cell is programmed to look out for this and when it picks up two languages it destroys the virus and the host cell. The other loophole is the American who just happens to speak English as well; all of the immune cells recognise this type of cell as self and leave it alone. The bug which causes syphilis is like this. The antigen or identity disc on its surface is the same as some of your heart muscle cells (cardiolipin). It can create havoc in the body without being checked for some time, until our army cottons on to the fact that it is doing damage. The immune cells then switch to destroying everything bearing that identity disc and so attack the heart muscle too . Fortunately, *Treponema,* the bug which does the damage, can now be destroyed with drugs, and as long as it is eliminated before the immune system recognises it, it need not cause heart problems.

Our cells obviously neither speak nor write, but they use amino acids where we would use letters and can therefore have amino acid identity discs. A cell which carries a *toes* or *ship* or *star* disc would be left alone in the body, being recognised as, for example, a heart, skin, or liver cell. Cells carrying *posl, foyq* or *qdbg* would be destroyed. It's a very clever system but like all systems it has its problems. One of the most common ones is a spelling mistake. If the body isn't working well, it could write stau instead of star. One error is o.k., the cell will be destroyed, but if *star* is replaced by *stau* on all the cells that should read star then an auto-immune disease could follow, where our own immune cells destroy our own body cells because their label is wrong.

Another problem is when the immune cells are overworked or not functioning well for some reason and make a mistake. The immune cells then also attack our own cells, erroneously thinking that *star* is not English.

All your cells are individuals on your star base. They all have their own name, function and needs. To stay healthy all these individuals have to live together in harmony. Unfortunately your star is constantly being bombarded by outside enemies and sometimes, when things get out of control, civil war breaks out as well, so our immune army needs all the help and co-operation it can get. Don't neglet your inner army. One day your life may depend on it. Next we'll be considering what different nutrients do for the immune system.

CHAPTER THREE

BOOSTING YOUR IMMUNE POWER

PROFESSOR John Yudkin (emeritus Professor of nutrition at London University) states that "The health of the majority of human beings depends more on their nutrition than it does on any other single factor". There is a lot of evidence to suggest that faulty nutrition is connected with many diseases. To improve our resistance to these there are four main areas of the diet which need to be looked at carefully.

Basis for an IMMUNE POWER diet

1. Eat mainly whole, unprocessed foods
2. Recognise and deal with food sensitivities
3. Rid your body of excess fat, and limit its intake
4. Balance food intake and supplement your diet as necessary, depending on individual intake, lifestyle, condition and needs.

1. Some advantages of whole, unprocessed foods
They come complete with most of the nutrients needed for their digestion. They provide complete, good quality building materials to make our bodies with. They provide a high-fibre

diet without having to add bran to everything, which can be an irritant to a sensitive gut and inhibits uptake of essential minerals. Eaten raw they provide many other factors (some of which are probably still unknown) like natural antibiotics, essential oils, pigments and enzymes, which are of benefit to health.

Raw, whole foods increase the oxygen content of our cells, especially important for the prevention of cancer, where cells have switched to live without oxygen. Fresh fruit and vegetables are high in potassium, which is essential for maintaining a healthy immune system and for avoiding cancer. We eat far too much sodium, in the form of salt, and not enough potassium to balance it.

Whole foods provide "time-released" sugar rather than the instant stuff provided by refined foods, which give an immediate high closely followed by a low which makes you feel hungry again faster.

All processed foods (and this even includes cooked wholefoods here) require your immune army to defend your gut and many white blood cells are lost. Raw foods, however, do not cause destruction of the white defenders. It would appear that some raw food, taken before cooked food, reduces or even eliminates battle fatalities, so saving you the energy used in fighting, repair and replacement.

The body knows exactly how to deal with natural whole foods, whereas some residues left by "chemical foods" can't be got rid of. They build up and have to be stored as safely as possible, somewhere.

2. What you eat strengthens or weakens your immune system

Every day we take foreign substances into our gut, substances which our immune system would react violently to if we injected them into the bloodstream or implanted them in the tissues. The IgA antibody which protects the gut is comparatively easy-going. However it does get upset when abused and we all abuse one food or another during our lives and so become sensitive to it. When we do our white blood cells slow down, swell and explode in their thousands, every time we come into contact with that food.

Ironically, it is the foods which we use all the time (and usually like a lot) that we become sensitive to; the milk which goes in tea or coffee throughout the day, every day, and wheat, our national addiction which goes into almost everything including pies, cakes, biscuits, breakfast cereals, snacks and soups.

We crave the foods that we are sensitive to because they trigger the release of *beta endorphins* which give you a high feeling and relieve that depression, anxiety, headache or other aches and pains which are probably present because you need another shot of your favourite addiction anyway. Another vicious circle.

Almost every symptom that you can imagine could be linked to a food sensitivity, especially if it is accompanied by loss of energy. Obviously, if your immune army is being destroyed by a lot of foods, your immune system is much weaker. If you can avoid most food sensitivities it will be stronger. The most common sensitive seven are wheat, dairy products, eggs, yeast, sugar, tea and coffee, because as a nation we tend to depend on these foods daily. You can become hooked on almost anything if you eat it often enough.

The best way to avoid food sensitivities is not to become dependent on any single foods, by rotating the diet in some way, either every 4 days, 4 weeks, or seasonally. Some people who suffer with food intolerance, eliminate the offending food only to replace it with another which they eat to excess and so become sensitive to that. Still others go from one sensitivity to another and end up eliminating almost everything, so adopting a dangerously narrow diet. This type of person has some other underlying cause such as candidiasis and should seek professional advice.

3. **FAT IS FOLLY, FIGHT IT**

Your immune system and your fat content are inextricably linked. If you have a weak immune system you may find it hard to maintain a normal body weight (gaining it if you are too thin or losing it if you're too fat). On the other hand, proving that life and the immune system are a heap of vicious circles, if you are carrying too much fat you are weakening the immune system.

Fatty acids are absorbed straight into the lympatic system. Too many make the lymph very heavy to push around, slow down your defenders and provide your attackers with more places to hide. One of the reasons for oedema (so-called water retention) is too much fat in the diet or too little exercise, which weakens the cells of the lymphatic vessels and causes them to leak. Fluid seeps out of these weakened areas and collects in the surrounding tissues, giving the characteristic swollen appearance usually at the extremities of your star points, i.e. head, hands and feet.

It is now common knowledge that excess fat taxes the heart and lungs, helps to block the arteries, weakens the liver, kidneys and hormonal system, as well as possibly promoting diabetes, cancer, and lowering resistance to infectious diseases. It is less well known that the immune system has several effects on our weight control. It regulates how we digest, absorb and store our food and how effectively we convert acquired nutrients into energy. The burning up of fat (as in weight loss) is dependent both on the status of the immune system and on having sufficient nutrients needed for the chemical reactions that turn food into energy.

The best way to lose weight is safely, slowly and sensibly. This can be done by gradually decreasing calories to 1,500 or 1,000, depending on height and activity and ensuring the correct balance of fat, protein, carbohydrate, as well as vitamins and minerals. It is best to avoid added saturated fat entirely during the slimming period (there will be plenty in the egg, cheese or meat portion). The essential fatty acids linoleic acid (in cold-pressed sunflower or safflower oils) or its next stage, GLA (in evening primrose oil or blackcurrant seed oil); and alpha linolenic acid or eicosapentaenoic acid (in seafoods and fish oils) should be added, as these are required for good immune function, in particular for antibody production.

The essential fatty acids are necessary, for although the body substitutes using saturated fat where it can, this isn't really the stuff for the job and years of unsatisfactory substitution finally takes its toll in the form of a weakened immune system and greater susceptibility to cancer, infectious, degenerative and autoimmune diseases.

To be able to adjust diet and supplements, it is necessary to know what the various nutrients do for the immune system.

NUTRIENTS THAT BOOST THE IMMUNE SYSTEM

Vitamin A is often totally used up during an infection and during this period of low A status, secondary infections can quickly take a hold. Insufficient A means that less lymphocytes will be made and those that are present have less ammunition, in the form of enzymes to fight with.

All cell walls are strengthened by vitamin A and weakened by a lack of it. This makes this vitamin important in the prevention of disease, because if cell walls are strong, would-be invading viruses which have to get inside your cells in order to multiply, cannot easily gain entry and may be destroyed by the rest of your immune army before they can do so.

Vitamin A promotes the growth of mucus-secreting cells and

so is of particular importance in the prevention and treatment of diseases of the respiratory, genito-urinary and alimentary tracts. Anyone who still smokes should seriously consider vitamin A supplementation as the diet cannot hope to keep up with the body's A requirements when so much is used up in repairing "smoke damage". Vitamin A is also effective at removing free radicals before they can do damage in the body.

Probably vitamin A's main role in maintaining the immune system is by maintaining activity of the thymus gland. This gland is our Ministry Of Defence's main computer, but it starts getting smaller from puberty. The slower we lose it the better, and vitamin A and sufficient zinc to utilise vitamin A as well as natural light (not through glass) , are important in maintaining the size and function of this gland.

You are likely to be deficient in this vitamin if you smoke, avoid fresh fruit, vegetables and fish, or suffer with ulcers, skin problems, thrush, respiratory problems or poor night vision. It can be taken as beta carotene, retinol, or in a synthetic form.

In our Western society, we tend to eat far too much protein. Vitamin A is synergistic with protein (they work together) hence the more protein we eat, the more vitamin A we need to maintain the correct balance. Vitamin A should not be consumed with alcohol as this combination can be toxic to the liver.

B-vitamins build better resistance

The B's are essential for an energetic, healthy, slim you. If they are deficient, your energy level goes down and so does your brain power. On top of that, if the deficiency is persistent, you lose emotional stability and control over body weight. There are many members of the B vitamin family: thiamine, Bl; riboflavin, B2; niacin, B3; pantothenic acid, B5; pyridoxine, B6; cobalamine, B12; orotic acid, B13; biotin; choline; and folic acid. Collectively they are known as the B Complex. They are usually found together naturally, and work best that way. Research has shown that if they are deficient there is lower antibody response, fewer immune cells and a shrinking of the immune organs.

B6 is particularly important as, on top of this, a deficiency causes a considerable decrease in phagocytic activity of macrophages and polymorphs, which means that we cannot get rid of germs or rubbish as effectively.

You are likely to be deficient in B's if you are taking medication, especially antibiotics and the pill, or if you suffer with PMT, depression, irritability and a lack of energy. Oedema occurs when the immune vessels are weak and the lymph fluid seeps out into the tissues where it is retained. B6 can help with prevention and treatment of this. We are often deficient in B6 these days as we tend to eat a lot of meat which uses up this vitamin during its digestion. It is also refined out of a lot of foods.

Folic acid is a B vitamin of crucial importance to the development of the immune system of the unborn child, along with the nutrients choline, B12 and methionine. It has been found that with a good maternal supply of these nutrients, the babies' immune systems are stronger and immune organs, especially the thymus, are larger.
Some people who cannot mount an effective immune response and are found to be folic acid deficient, can return to a normal immune response with supplementation. Folic acid is required by red blood cells and for detoxification of foreign chemicals such as pesticides and drugs. It should always be taken with B12.

Choline also deserves special mention, as when it is changed to a compound called dimethyl glycine, lymphocyte production is increased 3 or 4 times and toxic substances are rendered harmless by this natural detoxification agent.

Vitamin C has to be the most researched vitamin and appears , at present to have the most immune power.

It is antiviral and increases interferon activity in the body, so making it difficult for any virus to multiply. This is particularly important since some viruses, like the flu and common cold viruses, do not necessarily enter the blood stream, but spread from cell to cell in th mucus linings, so there is very little antibody production. This is one reason why it is diffficult to obtain vaccines effective against these viruses. Defence falls to T lymphocytes and the vitamin C levels in these T cells is crucial to their putting up a good fight. This level is often depleted with age and in the presence of infection or pollution, for example, smoking.

Vitamin C can also kill or slow down bacteria, and actually improves the action of antibodies when these are required. It is needed for the correct functioning of the T cells, in preventing premature aging and susceptability to inflammatory and heart disorders. It causes a rapid increase of white blood cells and, along with hydrogen peroxide and some metals, in particular zinc, is needed to make the weapons used to kill those enemies.

Histamine, a substance naturally produced in the body (which is often especially high in those prone to allergies) acts as an immunosuppressant. Vitamin C, being a natural antihistamine counteracts and alleviates some symptoms.

It can also prevent some carcinogenic chemicals from converting to their cancer inducing form, and detoxify some drugs and bacterial toxins.

You are likely to be deficient if you avoid fresh fruit and raw vegetables, live or work near busy traffic, suffer with frequent infections or bleeding gums and bruise easily.

Vitamin E

Sadly, with our present day obsession with increasing the shelf life of food, most of the vitamin E is removed from our diet: even those polyunsaturate oils which should be full of it have had it removed and replaced with artificial antioxidants.

Many authorities on the aging process suggest that it is the accumulative effect of *free radical* damage which is the root of premature aging and that the more severe the damage the more susceptible we are to the debilitating and degenerative diseases such as arthritis, diabetes, cancer and cardiovascular disease. Vitamin E is one of the best free radical deactivators that there is.

It will cancel out those free radicals as they are formed if there is enough of it. It also helps you maintain a strong fighting force and stimulates antibody production.

If you avoid whole grains and cold pressed oils and seeds, you are certain to be deficient.

THE MAGIC AND MENACE OF MINERALS

Zinc and the art of self-defence

Blood levels of zinc change dramatically in most disease states. They are always depressed in cancer patients. Zinc is anti-inflammatory and antibacterial and so helps in the management of inflammatory and infectious diseases, as well as wound healing (from spots to ulcers to surgery). It plays a major role in maintaining the size and activity of members of the immune system.

Zinc is of particular importance to the unborn baby as it is needed to ensure a large and active thymus and hence much better resistance to infections. Insufficient zinc at any stage in life means a decrease in activity of immune related organs.

Another crucial stage for zinc intake is around puberty, which is when our immune system starts to age!

Zinc is present in over 200 enzymes used in the body, many of which are used by the immune system. The hormone , thymulin, which is necessary for maturation of T lymphocytes is also dependent on zinc. Soil and hence vegetable levels are low in this country, so almost all of us could do with a bit extra, but especially adolescents, pregnant women and men with high sexual activity (zinc is lost in seminal fluid).

Iron deficiency is common today, especially in children, pregnant or menstruating women and vegetarians. It is often possible to iron out a few immune wrinkles with iron, however it is also easy to overdose as too much is actually bad for the immune system. Iron in food has low toxicity so iron rich foods are preferable to supplements. Taking vitamin C generally enhances its absorption from food. The right amount of iron boosts overall resistance to infection, and is essential for antibody production and for digesting and killing enzymes produced by macrophages and pmn's. There is also an iron containing enzyme, *myeloperoxidase*, which is used to make white blood cells. Iron can also help with the detoxification of some drugs and bacterial toxins.

Bacteria, however, love iron and when we are infected with pathogenic bacteria, the white blood cells have to release an iron binding protein called ferrolactin so that any spare iron that we might have cannot be used by these bugs. An iron supplement is obviously not a good idea if you have a bacterial infection.

Selenium is a mineral we need very little of compared with other nutrients. Our daily requirement is around 50mcg, which, for example, is a millionth of our daily protein needs. But Britain has one of the lowest soil levels of this element so we could all do with a little more, however too much selenium is toxic and recommended doses should not be exceeded without professional advice. Along with vitamin E, selenium is essential for antibody production and studies have, shown that there is no antibody production at all in animals that are deprived of both. It has also been suggested that, if given at the time of vaccination, vitamin E and selenium increase antibody production. White blood cells need it and appear to loose the ability to recognise invaders without it.

Calcium is needed by phagocytic cells in order to attach to, ingest and digest foreign material. Cytotoxic T cells also require calcium. Without it they cannot destroy viruses once they've entered your cells. Complement cannot complete its jig-saw without calcium. These are your three main methods of defence, without which you have a very limited immune army.

Calcium is needed for fever production. There are many advantages of a slightly raised temperature when you have an infection. Macrophages move faster and produce enzymes which kill faster. Some viruses cannot replicate at elevated temperature, while others cannot function at all. We need a lot of calcium in the diet. It isn't toxic.

Magnesium is a common element in the earth and in our bodies. Perhaps because of this it has been taken for granted that we have enough of it, in reality, however, the magnesium content of our bodies has gone down by almost 50% in the last 40 years.

Calcium, magnesium and phosphorous need to be in balance. Our fast food and drinks provide ample phosphorus and many people eat a lot of dairy products to get their calcium. However poor magnesium usually gets forgotten, although it is needed for proper calcium absorption. It is found in nuts,

Molybdenum is a mineral few people have heard of. It is essential for man. Deficiency of molybdenum is associated with fatigue, infertility and cancer. Like selenium, it is required for enzymes that are involved in oxidation. It is likely that its role in cancer prevention will become established in the next five years. Molybdenum is found in pulses and grains. It is highest in buckwheat, wheatgerm, lima beans, navy beans, soya beans and barley.

Copper is an essential metal, needed by many enzyme systems, including some of those used by the immune system. We need sufficient copper to raise an effective immune response, but these days we usually have excess rather than a deficiency. This can lead to symptoms of zinc deficiency as these two need to be balanced.

MONSTER MINERALS

Not all elements are required by the body. In fact some interfere with it and so are termed *anti-nutrients*. Antinutrients always have a detrimental effect on the immune system either directly or because they interfere with the uptake of nutritional minerals. Calcium, iron, magnesium, selenium and zinc are often pushed out by toxic bullies like aluminium, arsenic, cadmium, lead. mercury and nickel.

Although nickel and arsenic are used in minute amounts our problem is always excess. Smoking and heavy margarine consumption contribute to nickel overload while chocolate, beer, shellfish and meat may contain arsenic if the raw material from which they are made (or fed) was sprayed with arsenic based insecticides.

The body often has no choice but to accept aluminium, cadmium, lead and mercury, although they can only do harm. A good analogy is that they are like keys which fit the locks of some of our enzyme systems but unlike the nutritional key which fits the lock and opens the door, the anti-nutrient key merely fills the lock so that the proper key can't be put in, but will not open the door. It is important to always maintain enough nutritional minerals so that they can fill the locks and open the doors first. We cannot totally avoid ant-inutrients but we can keep them to a minimum.

Flouride fools the immune system. Small quantities slow down, weaken and confuse the body's major defenders, it alters the shape of protein and the cells that seek and destroy no longer recognise the altered proteins as self and so attack them. The presence of flouride induces the release of free radicals in resting white cells thereby causing weapons to be released when they are not needed. Ironically it inhibits their release when they are needed to destroy invaders.

SUPPLEMENTS FOR IMMUNE STRENGTH

It is always preferable to get what we need from whole, natural food sources, however, nowadays there are gaps that do need filling with supplements. Why?

1. We are not as active as our ancestors, so we need less food but not less nutrients.
2. We actually need more nutrients to balance all those anti-nutrients that we are now forced to consume due to pollution, artificial chemical additives, sprays etc.
3. The soil is low in some of the minerals that we require and would normally expect to get from it, via plants and other animals; zinc and selenium, being prime examples here.
4. Nutrients are destroyed by our storing, cooking and processing methods.
5. Everyone has their own likes and dislikes, and this can lead to nutritional imbalances.
6. Unnatural habits and conditions like smoking or surgery require such a lot of some nutrients that one could not possibly get enough from food.
7. Stress, illness, pregnancy and puberty all demand extra nutritional requirements.

Supplements are necessary for modern day living but doses vary depending on the individual's circumstances. They need revising every now and then.

Most people would benefit from a basic daily supplement containing:- Vitamin A 7,500mg: Vitamin B complex 50-75mg base; Vitamin C 1gm; Vitamin D 400iu; Vit E 100iu; Zinc 15mg; Selenium, 50mcg; Chromium, 30mcg; Magnesium, 150mg; Calcium, 150mg; Manganese, 5mg; Iron 2mg, as well as some dietary cold pressed safflower or sunflower oil for essential fatty acids.

However, if you are prone to infections you may benefit from more vitamin A, C, E, zinc and selenium on a daily basis. A good multivitamin is Health+Plus's *VV Pack*, taken together with *Immunade*, a supplement containing all these immune boosting nutrients.

People with specific symptoms should seek professional advice with a nutritionist as this may not be sufficient for them or they may have a particular imbalance which requires attention.

SUPPLEMENTS TO FIGHT INFECTION

If you were too late boosting and have clear early warning signs of a cold or other infection, try to work with your immune system for a speedier recovery. Rest, when possible ; don't eat unless you really want to (and if you do eat the right thing, and drink plenty of water); allow any fever to take it's course, rather than suppressing it; and take the supplements with plenty of fluid. You will need more Vitamin C as most animals make their own and always increase their supply several fold when ill, but we have lost the ability to do this. Do remember to decrease the dose gradually when you have recovered.

These supplements are compatible with antibiotics - in fact vitamin C enhances their action. After a course of antibiotics it is wise to supplement B vitamins and to take yoghourt or Lactobacillus acidophilus supplements to put back the gut bacteria which will have been killed, otherwise the fungus that causes thrush may proliferate and give problems.

POINTS OF CAUTION

One should not take too much more than 15,000iu vitamin A in the retinol (non-vegetarian) form 50mg vitamin B6 when pregnant. Professional advice should be sought if there is any medical condition as supplementation could alter the amount of drug needed (eg. a diabetic may need less insulin). Anyone with heart problems should increase Vitamin E gradually, 50-100iu at a time and should also be cautious with vitamin D. There are many medical conditions which alter your nutritional requirements, but in those circumstances personal advice is required. Nutritional therapy is intended to meet the needs of the individual person as a whole not merely to treat any condition which he or she may have.

SUPPLEMENT BOOST

So here's what to increase when you're fighting an infection:

Vitamin A as beta carotene *increase to 25,000iu*
Vitamin C *increase daily supplement by 2 or 3 gms, as a divided dose.*
VItamin E *increase by 400iu*
Zinc *increase up to 50mg*
Calcium *increase up to 600mg*
Magnesium *increase up to 300mg*
Selenium *increase up to 200mcg*

Immunade, a supplement made by Health+Plus is a good immune boosting supplement to keep in stock for such occasions along with extra vitamin C. One a day provides 7,500iu of vitamin A in the retinol form and 12,500iu of beta-carotene. It also provides 1gm of vitamin C, 100iu of vitamin E, 20mg of zinc, 100mcg of selenium, 150mg of both calcium and magnesium and 50mcg of molybdenum. Two or three a day provides maximum support for your immune system when engaged in battle.

Remember your defence depends on maintaining a strong, well equipped immune army all of the time and your quick action if an attack is threatened. It's no good waiting until you've used half a box of tissues before you decide to get boosting. Your battle advantage will have been lost.

WHAT HAPPENS WHEN WE GET SICK?

When you are ill, your energy level drops, All energy which can be diverted goes to the immune army. Limbs ache or feel heavy, because all available calcium and magnesium go to aid defence. There are often digestion problems as again energy is diverted to the immune system, leaving only the minimum to digest food. There is usually loss of appetite but, for some strange reason we force food into ourselves in the mistaken belief that it gives energy, whereas in actual fact it takes energy from our fighting force. There is weight loss because we use body stores for energy, not immediately digested food. When we recover from an illness, appetite is often greater than usual and this is the time to eat and return body supplies used up during the illness. The tongue is often coated and skin condition deteriorates as this is a major site for removal of toxins formed on the battlefield.

There is often a fever because this helps the immune system do its job as long as the body remains in control and the temperature doesn't go dangerously high.

WHY DO WE GET SICK?

There is an underlying purpose for everything, including sickness, and the usual purpose of physical or mental pain, is to draw attention to conditions of disharmony in the body, which require correction.

Sickness, in body language is an attempt to warn us of an attack, usually from external forces, like germs, which demand our attention and extra supplies of defenders and weapons; or that we are doing something wrong which is causing us to malfunction. Stress, inappropriate exercise, eating solely for pleasure and disregarding need are examples of lifestyles which will cause dis-ease in a body. The resulting symptoms of disease are often caused by the body trying to correct itself, but we help or hinder restoration of the natural balance.

COPING WITH INFECTIOUS DISEASES

Disease causing bugs are around us all of the time, we cannot avoid them; what makes us all different is how we overcome them. Problems occur when an individual's immune system is too weak to fight back or when, for example, someone sneezes directly over you, so showering you with a whole army in one shot!

CATCH A COLD BEFORE IT CATCHES YOU!

If you think you're starting a cold don't wait for that invading army to attack, boost your weapons of war and eliminate it before it has a chance to actually get inside your cells and make further reinforcements. Be aware of close contacts with infected people and also of your own initial symptoms and always act immediately if you feel that you could be invaded. Nutritional immune boosters, taken unnecessarily, just in case , or in response to a false alarm will give you expensive urine but won't do any harm. If they prevent or soften an attack they will save you a lot of discomfort.

WHAT ABOUT FOOD?

When you think about it, nature has the perfect system cracked. It provides foods in seasonal rotation , so that we do not become sensitive to them, and it provides foods packed with immune power boosters in the autumn, which we, in this country, need before winter, when we have less stimulation of our immune system from natural sunlight, and when the cold and flu bugs traditionally play "hunt the human". At harvest our food has high vitamin content this gradually decreases with time so that we are weaned off slowly as spring arrives and we need less.

MAN KNOWS BEST - OR THINKS HE DOES

1. Seasonal food is now available all year round, we either preserve it or import it.
2. Man has been obsessed with storing food, it can now be stored for so long that there are few, if any micronutrients left.
3. Nutrients are often specially taken out of food, by various processing methods to increase the shelf life, after all, no self respecting bug would want to eat deficient foods, when given a choice they will eat whole foods, so making them go bad first and leave the processed stuff for those intellectually superior humans.
4. We spray foods with various pesticides to stop other things from eating our precious stores, regardless of the fact that many of these poison us too. Others, like methyl bromide and some of the chlorinated hydrocarbons completely destroy all of the vitamin B5 and inositol respectively.
5. The soil and crops are covered with so many chemicals that wise worms wriggle long distances to pop into the organic farm nest door.
6. The worth of a pound of human flesh has increased, in money terms, in that we have increased our lead, mercury, aluminium, cadmium and nickel content considerably in recent years. In terms of body function, the increase in these and others has made us worth significantly less.

TAKE THE CONSEQUENCES - OR REAP THE REWARDS

We have to take the consequences of many imbalances that we bring upon ourselves. To every action there is an equal and opposite reaction, this is a basic law for all life, known as the law of Karma, (we often try to ignore it's wider application by filing it away in the physical sciences as Newton's 3rd law of motion). As we can only reap what we sow, we need to correct some of those imbalances if we are to minimise premature aging and degenerative disease which often manifest themselves in the autumn of life.

It is difficult to convince apparently healthy, symptom free people to change the lifestyle and diet they enjoy, but it is possible to change gradually and to be just as happy with healthier eating habits, and so also to reap the rewards of an active healthy autumn and winter of life.

The immune system is our Achilles heal, as it is the first system in the body to deteriorate. It is overworked and underpaid in terms of materials needed for it to function optimally.

We pile more and more rubbish into ourselves and expect the immune system to deal with it, even though we have made drastic cuts in labour and equipment for cleaning up the operation.

A lot of time and money is spent on dress, appearance and external hygiene but we choose to ignore the putrifying waste within. It's time for a "Keep Body Internally Tidy" campaign.

Eat less. There's lots of interesting things to do in all that time that used to be spent eating! Words written in an Egyptian pyramid 5,000 years ago still apply today, they are,"Man lives on one quarter of what he eats. His doctor lives on the other three quarters".

Make sure that food you eat is real food, not just a bag of chemically laden, empty calories, and make up with supplements when neccessary.

Splash out on pampering your immune system, encourage it and don't let it become overworked that it becomes confused and starts making mistakes, after all, life is for living and who wants to waste time being sick?

USEFUL ADDRESSES

THE AUTHOR is a practising nutritionist and lecturer. For consultations please ring or write to Jennifer Meek, 58 Tollerford Road, West Camford Heath, Poole, DORSET Tel:0202 690428.

HEALTH+PLUS vitamin company supply vitamin and mineral supplements, including Immunade, by mail order. Ring or write to Health+Plus, Health+Plus House, 118 Station Road, Chinnor, OXON OX9 4EZ Tel:0844 52098.

THE INSTITUTE FOR OPTIMUM NUTRITION offers courses and personal consultations with trained nutritionists, including Jennifer Meek. A directory of ION-trained nutritionists is available for £1. To receive ION's information pack please ring or write to ION, 5 Jerdan Place, London SW6 1BE Tel:01 385 7984.

RECOMMENDED READING

The following books will help you dig deeper into nutrition and immunity.

Dr Theron Randolph - *Allergies: Your Hidden Enemy* (Thorsons). An excellent introduction to food allergy, what it is and how to reduce your allergic potential.

Patrick Holford - *Vitamin Vitality* (ION Press) 1985. A thoroughly researched book which establishes why so many people are sub-optimally nourished and how to work out your own vitamin and mineral needs for optimum health.

Michael Weiner - *Maximum Immunity* (Gateway Books) 1986. A good book for those who want to dig deeper into immunity.

Drs Stephen Davies and Alan Stewart - *Nutritional Medicine* (Pan) 1987. An authoritative guide, packed full of practical tips for applying optimum nutrition in practice.

INDEX

Adrenal gland 17
aging 8,34,36,45
AIDS 8, 23
aluminium 38
antibiotics 33, 40
antibody 20, 21, 23, 29, 32, 34, 35, 36, 37
antigen 21, 28-29
antioxidant 35
appendix 17
arsenic 38
autoimmunity 24-25

Babies 33
bacteria 8,14, 22, 23, 34, 36
balance 10
blood 12,17, 18, 19, 22, 28, 34
blood cells red 18, 33
white 18-21, 28, 29, 34, 37, 39

Cadmium 38, 44
calcium 22, 37, 38, 40, 41
cancer 8,11, 21, 28, 30, 31, 34, 35, 37, 38
carbohydrate 13
choline 33
chromium 40
cold, common 43
complement 22, 37
copper 38

Depression 11, 15, 29
diet 27-31
disease 23,31

Energy 14, 28, 29, 42
enzymes 19, 21, 22, 23, 31, 36, 37, 38
essential fatty acids 13, 31, `34, 40

exercise 8,10, 11, 12, 13, 14, 43

Fat 12,13, 27, 30-31
fever 37, 40, 42
flu 23, 34, 43
fluoride 39
folic acid 33
food sensitivities 9, 14, 27-30
free radicals 32, 35, 39
fruit 14, 28, 32, 34

Genito-urinary tract 21, 31-32
grains 38
gut 21, 29, 32

Histamine 34
hormones 11, 12

Illness 21, 39, 40, 42-43
immunade 41
immune cells 10. 18-21, 24, 31, 33
immuno-suppressants 11, 34
infection 8,17, 31, 34, 35, 36
inflammatory disorders 9, 34, 35, 45
interferons 21, 22, 34
intestines 17
iron 36, 38, 40

Lactobacillus 40
law of life 44
lead 38, 44
liver 17
lymphatic system 10, 17, 18, 19, 30, 33
lymphocytes B 18, 21-22, 23, 31, 33
T 18-21, 23, 24, 31, 33-34, 37

INDEX

lysosomes 1, 19, 22

Macrophage 18, 19, 20, 21, 22, 33, 36, 37
magnesium 22, 37, 38, 40, 41
manganese 22, 40
mercury 38, 44
mind 11, 12
molybdenum 37, 41
mucus membranes 22, 31-32, 34
myeloperoxidase 36

Nickel 38, 44
nutrients 27-39
nuts 37

Oedema 30,33

Pesticides 38, 44, 89
phagocytosis 19, 21, 33
phosphorous 37
pill, the 33
pituitary 17
pollution 8,9, 39
polymorph 18, 19, 20, 21, 22, 33, 36
potassium 28
protein 13, 32

Respiratory tract 21, 31-32

Salt 12, 28
seeds 37
selenium 36, 38, 39, 40, 41
skin 12, 15, 22, 42
sleep 11, 14
smoke 8, 14, 32, 34, 38, 39
spleen 17
stress 8, 13, 39, 43
sugar 28
supplements 13, 14, 36, 39, 40

Thrush 8, 40
thymus 17, 20, 23, 32, 33, 35
tonsils 17
toxins 22, 32, 33, 34, 36

Unhappiness 8, 11, 14

Vaccination 23, 34, 37
vegetables 14, 28, 32, 34, 37
virus 8, 14, 20, 21, 22, 31, 34, 37
vitamins A 31-32, 40, 41
B 12, 32-33, 40, 41, 44
C 22, 23, 34, 36, 40, 41
D 40, 41
E 35, 40, 41

Weight control 30-32

Zinc 22, 32, 34, 35-36, 38, 39, 40, 41